This Journal Belongs To:

Made in the USA
Monee, IL
14 September 2021

78029937R00057